GUITAR
CHORDS
MADE EASY

mobile
online
in print

Flame Tree Music
BOOKS • eBOOKS • RESOURCES

Publisher and Creative Director: Nick Wells
Project, design and media integration: Jake Jackson
Website and software: David Neville with Stevens Dumpala and Steve Moulton
Editorial: Laura Bulbeck, Emma Chafer and Esme Chapman

Special thanks to: Jane Ashley, Frances Bodiam, Helen Crust,
Christine Delaborde, Stephen Feather, Sara Robson, Chris Herbert, Polly Prior,
Gail Sharkey, Mike Spender and Birgitta Williams.

First published 2013 by
FLAME TREE PUBLISHING
Crabtree Hall, Crabtree Lane
Fulham, London SW6 6TY
United Kingdom

www.flametreepublishing.com

Music information site: www.flametreemusic.com

15 17 16 14
3 5 7 9 10 8 6 4

The CIP record for this book is available from the British Library.

Android is a trademark of Google Inc. Logic Pro, iPhone and iPad are either registered trademarks or trademarks of
Apple Computer Inc. in the United States and/or other countries. Cubase is a registered trademark or trademark of
Steinberg Media Technologies GmbH, a wholly owned subsidiary of Yamaha Corporation, in the United States and/or
other countries. Nokia's product names are either trademarks or registered trademarks of Nokia. Nokia is a registered
trademark of Nokia Corporation in the United States and/or other countries. Samsung and Galaxy S are both
registered trademarks of Samsung Electronics America, Ltd. in the United States and/or other countries.

Jake Jackson is a writer and musician. He has created and contributed to over 20 practical music books,
including *Reading Music Made Easy*, *Play Flamenco* and *Piano and Keyboard Chords*. His music is available
on iTunes, Amazon and Spotify amongst others.

ISBN: 978-0-85775-798-2

Printed in China

GUITAR CHORDS MADE EASY

SEE IT ◼ HEAR IT

COMPREHENSIVE SOUND LINKS

JAKE JACKSON

FLAME TREE
PUBLISHING

Contents

Guitar Chords
An Introduction

Chord Diagrams
A Quick Guide

The Sound Links
A Quick Guide

The Website
flametreemusic.com

The Chords

A
A#/B♭
B
C
C#/D♭
D
D#/E♭
E
F
F#/G♭
G
G#/A♭

FREE ACCESS on smartphones including iPhone & Android   Using any QR code app scan and **HEAR** the chord (e.g. this is C Major).

Guitar Chords
An Introduction

Chords are the building blocks for every budding musician. Stringing together a few triads can liberate a melody and, being easy to communicate, will help you play with others. GUITAR CHORDS MADE EASY combines a solid approach to chord diagrams with an integrated, online sound solution.

When I first started to play the guitar I bought a cheap steel-string acoustic, an **Epiphone**. I saw it in the window of a guitar shop I passed every day. It was surrounded by more glamorous instruments, mainly electic-blue **Fender Strats** and sunburst **Gibson Les Pauls**. But, at the price, I loved the look of it – the full body, the slim neck – and eventually saved up enough money to buy it, stealing myself for the inevitable complaints from my neighbours.

It didn't go well at first. In later years I came to realize that the cheaper the guitar, the harder they are to play, but at the time the strings were so far off the neck I could barely press them down and I suffered weeks of physical agony, nearly giving up. But I had a friend and he had a heavy wooden guitar, a beast, a **Westone Thunder**. I watched his impossibly big fingers float across the frets as he made the music dance, so he kept me inspired. And he was patient; oh, boy was he patient.

Eventually I *could* press down the strings, and continued with some simple chords, E minor, A minor, I think, and a top-three-string G major and a D major. Well, it's incredible how many songs can come from just these four chords! Of course I tried loads of chord books. A decent one is not ashamed of its reader because simplicity is essential at any level. You

FREE ACCESS on smartphones
including iPhone & Android

Using any QR code app scan and
HEAR the chord (e.g. this is C Major).

6

want to see the chord, understand it quickly and play it (I still do!). Of course the more you play, the more curious you get. And, when you're looking for new sounds, a new feel always comes from a new chord: it's very useful to explore the 6ths and the 9ths, and when your fingers are warm and loose, try some of the 7sus4s and 11ths, or 13ths. In the early days, I used to have a songwriting rule: *every new tune would contain something new*, for me, sometimes it was a rhythm, sometimes a new verse/ chorus structure, but most often, it was a **new chord**. Using a new set of notes can spring life into a tired bag of basic chords and force your developing musical brain into new territory.

So, chords are important to every songwriter, but especially for anyone playing with others, arranging and working out chord progressions. This new book offers just the first position on **20 chords per key**. It gives you a great range to experiment with and, combined with the power of mobile technology, you can **hear** how the chord is meant to sound by using a **smartphone** and any **free QR reader app**. Connected to the flametreemusic.com website you can hear each chord (on the piano and the keyboard) and a second guitar position too.

This is such a great tool, a unique experience that will give you hours of productive fun, whether you're bashing out some great songs, or playing with others. **Good Luck!**

Jake Jackson, London

A
A#/Bb
B
C
C#/Db
D
D#/Eb
E
F
F#/Gb
G
G#/Ab

Chord Diagrams
A Quick Guide

The chord diagrams are designed for quick access and ease of use. You can flick through book using the tabs on the side to find the right key, then use the finger positions and fretboard to help you make the chord.

Each chord is provided with a *Chord Spelling* to help you check each note. This is a great way to learn the structure of the sounds you are making and will help with melodies and solo work.

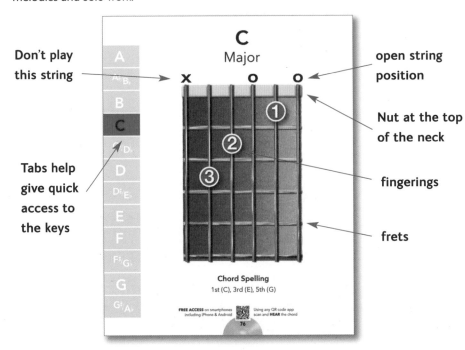

Don't play this string

open string position

Nut at the top of the neck

Tabs help give quick access to the keys

fingerings

frets

C
Major

Chord Spelling
1st (C), 3rd (E), 5th (G)

FREE ACCESS on smartphones including iPhone & Android — Using any QR code app scan and HEAR the chord

76

FREE ACCESS on smartphones including iPhone & Android

Using any QR code app scan and **HEAR** the chord (e.g. this is C Major).

Title: Each chord is given a short and complete name, for example the short name C°7 is properly known as C Diminished 7th.

The Strings: The bass E appears on the left, the top E is on the right (The top E is the E above middle C on the piano).

Fingerings: ❶ is the index finger   ❷ is the middle finger
❸ is the ring finger   ❹ is the little finger

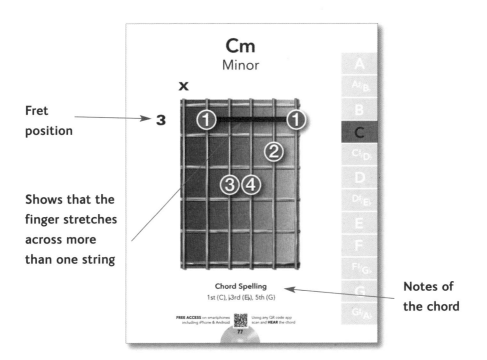

Fret position

Shows that the finger stretches across more than one string

Notes of the chord

The Sound Links
A Quick Guide

Requirements: a camera and internet ready smartphone (eg. **iPhone**, any **Android** phone (e.g. **Samsung Galaxy**), **Nokia Lumia**, or **camera-enabled tablet** such as the **iPad Mini**). The best result is achieved using a WIFI connection.

1. Download any **free QR code reader**. An app store search will reveal a great many of these, so obviously its is best to go with the ones with the highest ratings and don't be afraid to try a few before you settle on the one that works best for you. Tapmedia's QR Reader app is good, or ATT Scanner (used below) or QR Media. Some of the free apps have ads, which can be annoying.

2. Find the chord you want to play, look at the diagram then check out the **QR code** at the base of the page.

FREE ACCESS on smartphones including iPhone & Android Using any QR code app scan and **HEAR** the chord

76

3. On your smartphone, open the app and **scan** the **QR code** at the base of any particular chord page.

4. The QR reader app will take you to a browser, then the specific chord will be displayed on the flametreemusic.com website.

FREE ACCESS on smartphones including iPhone & Android Using any QR code app scan and **HEAR** the chord (e.g. this is C Major).

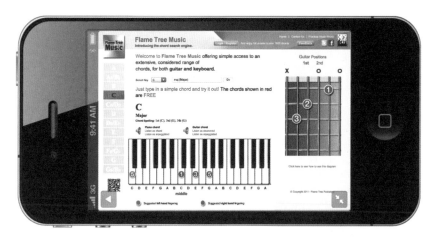

5. Using the usual pinch and zoom techniques, you can focus on four sound options.

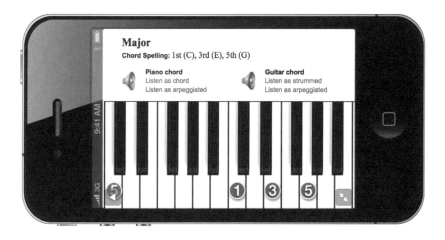

6. Click the sounds! Both piano and guitar audio is provided. This is particularly helpful when you're playing with others.

The QR codes give you direct access to all the chords. You can access a much wider range of chords if you register and subscribe.

FREE ACCESS on smartphones including iPhone & Android

Using any QR code app scan and **HEAR** the chord (e.g. this is C Major).

The Website
flametreemusic.com

The Flame Tree Music website is designed to make searching for chords very easy. It complements our range of print publications and offers easy access to chords online and on the move, through tablets, smartphones, desktop computers and books.

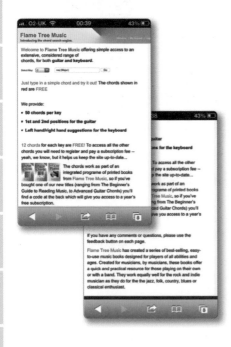

1. The site offers access to chord diagrams and finger positions for both the guitar and the piano/keyboard, presenting a wide range of sound options to help develop good listening technique, and to assist you in identifying the chord and each note within it.

2. The site offers 12 **free** chords, those most commonly used in a band setting or in songwriting.

3. A subscription is available for those who would like access to the full range of chords, **50** for **each key**.

FREE ACCESS on smartphones including iPhone & Android

Using any QR code app scan and **HEAR** the chord (e.g. this is C Major).

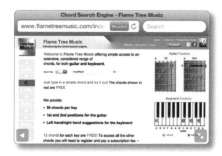

4. Guitar chords are shown with **first** and **second positions**.

5. For the keyboard, **left-** and **right-hand positions** are shown. The keyboard also sounds each note.

6. Choose the key, then the chord name from the drop down menu. Note that the **red chords** are available **free**. Those in blue can be accessed with a subscription.

7. Once you've selected the chord, press **GO** and the details of the chord will be shown, with chord spellings, keyboard and guitar fingerings.

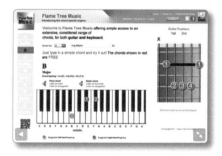

8. Initially, the first position for the guitar is shown. The second position can be selected by clicking the text above the chord diagram.

9. Sounds are provided in four easy-to-understand configurations.

The website is constantly evolving, so further features will be added, including resources, scales and modes.

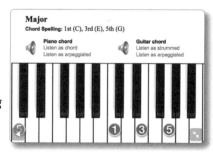

A

A#/B♭

B

C

C#/D♭

D

D#/E♭

E

F

F#/G♭

G

G#/A♭

The Chords

FREE ACCESS on smartphones
including iPhone & Android

Using any QR code app scan and
HEAR the chord (e.g. this is C Major).

A

A#/B♭

B

C

C#/D♭

D

D#/E♭

E

F

F#/G♭

G

G#/A♭

A
Major

A#/Bb

B

C

C#/Db

D

D#/Eb

E

F

F#/Gb

G

G#/Ab

Chord Spelling
1st (A), 3rd (C#), 5th (E)

FREE ACCESS on smartphones including iPhone & Android

Using any QR code app scan and **HEAR** the chord

Am
Minor

Chord Spelling
1st (A), ♭3rd (C), 5th (E)

A

A#/B♭

B

C

C#/D♭

D

D#/E♭

E

F

F#/G♭

G

G#/A♭

A+
Augmented Triad

A
A#/Bb
B
C
C#/Db
D
D#/Eb
E
F
F#/Gb
G
G#/Ab

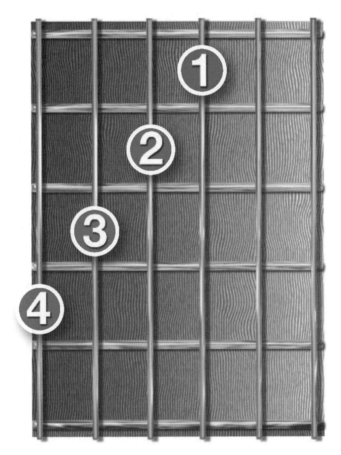

X   X

2

① ② ③ ④

Chord Spelling
1st (A), 3rd (C#), #5th (E#)

A°
Diminished Triad

X   O   X

Chord Spelling
1st (A), ♭3rd (C), ♭5th (E♭)

Asus2
Suspended 2nd

A

A#/Bb

B

C

C#/Db

D

D#/Eb

E

F

F#/Gb

G

G#/Ab

Chord Spelling
1st (A), 2nd (B), 5th (E)

Asus4
Suspended 4th

Chord Spelling
1st (A), 4th (D), 5th (E)

A5
5th (Power Chord)

A
A#/Bb
B
C
C#/Db
D
D#/Eb
E
F
F#/Gb
G
G#/Ab

Chord Spelling
1st (A), 5th (E)

A6
Major 6th

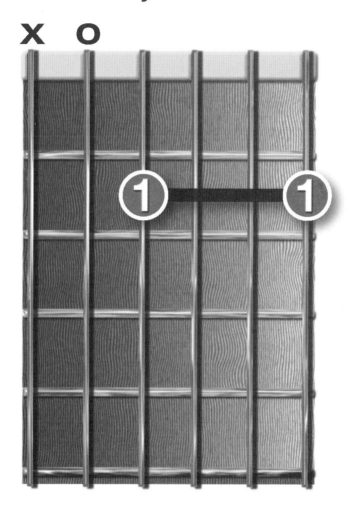

Chord Spelling
1st (A), 3rd (C#), 5th (E), 6th (F#)

A
A#/Bb
B
C
C#/Db
D
D#/Eb
E
F
F#/Gb
G
G#/Ab

Am6

Minor 6th

Chord Spelling

1st (A), b3rd (C), 5th (E), 6th (F#)

A6sus4
6th Suspended 4th

X O

Chord Spelling
1st (A), 4th (D), 5th (E), 6th (F#)

Amaj7
Major 7th

Chord Spelling
1st (A), 3rd (C#), 5th (E), 7th (G#)

A
A#/Bb
B
C
C#/Db
D
D#/Eb
E
F
F#/Gb
G
G#/Ab

Am7
Minor 7th

X   O   O   O

Chord Spelling
1st (A), ♭3rd (C), 5th (E), ♭7th (G)

A
A♯/B♭
B
C
C♯/D♭
D
D♯/E♭
E
F
F♯/G♭
G
G♯/A♭

FREE ACCESS on smartphones
including iPhone & Android

Using any QR code app
scan and **HEAR** the chord

A7
Dominant 7th

A
A#/Bb
B
C
C#/Db
D
D#/Eb
E
F
F#/Gb
G
G#/Ab

Chord Spelling
1st (A), 3rd (C#), 5th (E), b7th (G)

A°7
Diminished 7th

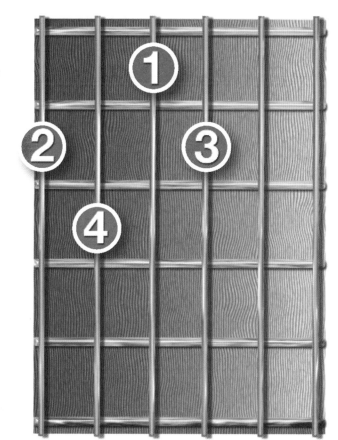

X X

4

① ② ③ ④

Chord Spelling
1st (A), ♭3rd (C), ♭5th (E♭), ♭♭7th (G♭)

A7sus4
Dominant 7th Suspended 4th

Chord Spelling
1st (A), 4th (D), 5th (E), ♭7th (G)

A

A#/B♭

B

C

C#/D♭

D

D#/E♭

E

F

F#/G♭

G

G#/A♭

Amaj9
Major 9th

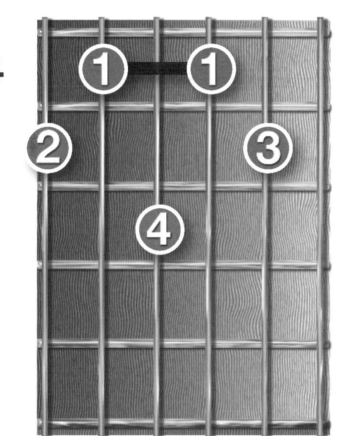

4

X

Chord Spelling
1st (A), 3rd (C#), 5th (E), 7th (G#), 9th (B)

Am9
Minor 9th

Chord Spelling
1st (A), ♭3rd (C), 5th (E), ♭7th (G), 9th (B)

FREE ACCESS on smartphones
including iPhone & Android

Using any QR code app
scan and **HEAR** the chord

A9
Dominant 9th

Chord Spelling
1st (A), 3rd (C♯), 5th (E), ♭7th (G), 9th (B)

A

A♯/B♭

B

C

C♯/D♭

D

D♯/E♭

E

F

F♯/G♭

G

G♯/A♭

Amaj11
Major 11th

Chord Spelling
1st (A), 3rd (C♯), 5th (E), 7th (G♯), 9th (B), 11th (D)

Amaj13
Major 13th

X O

Chord Spelling
1st (A), 3rd (C#), 5th (E), 7th (G#), 9th (B), 11th (D), 13th (F#)

FREE ACCESS on smartphones including iPhone & Android

Using any QR code app scan and **HEAR** the chord

A♯/B♭
Major

A

A♯/B♭

B

C

C♯/D♭

D

D♯/E♭

E

F

F♯/G♭

G

G♯/A♭

Chord Spelling
1st (B♭), 3rd (D), 5th (F)

A♯/B♭m
Minor

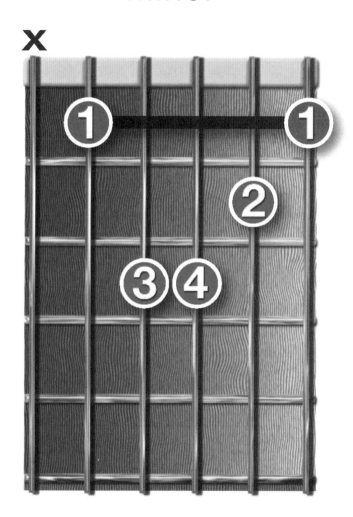

Chord Spelling
1st (B♭), ♭3rd (D♭), 5th (F)

A

A♯/B♭

B

C

C♯/D♭

D

D♯/E♭

E

F

F♯/G♭

G

G♯/A♭

A♯/B♭+

Augmented Triad

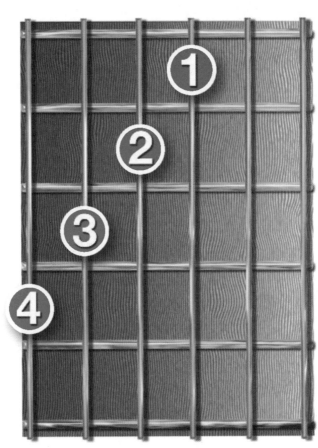

3

X X

Chord Spelling

1st (B♭), 3rd (D), ♯5th (F♯)

A

A♯/B♭

B

C

C♯/D♭

D

D♯/E♭

E

F

F♯/G♭

G

G♯/A♭

A♯/B♭°
Diminished Triad

X ... **O**

① ② ③ ④

A
A♯/B♭
B
C
C♯/D♭
D
D♯/E♭
E
F
F♯/G♭
G
G♯/A♭

Chord Spelling
1st (B♭), ♭3rd (D♭), ♭5th (F♭)

A♯/B♭sus2
Suspended 2nd

Chord Spelling
1st (B♭), 2nd (C), 5th (F)

A#/B♭sus4
Suspended 4th

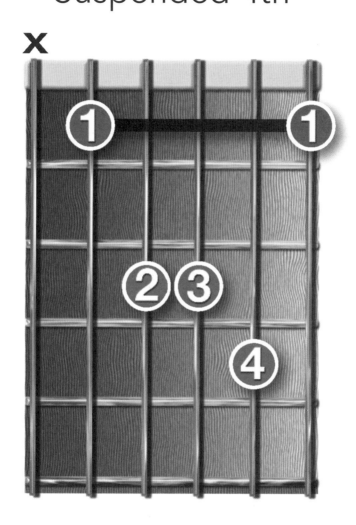

Chord Spelling
1st (B♭), 4th (E♭), 5th (F)

A

A#/B♭

B

C

C#/D♭

D

D#/E♭

E

F

F#/G♭

G

G#/A♭

A#/B♭5
5th (Power Chord)

A#/B♭

Chord Spelling
1st (B♭), 5th (F)

A#/Bb6
Major 6th

Chord Spelling
1st (Bb), 3rd (D), 5th (F), 6th (G)

A♯/B♭m6

Minor 6th

Chord Spelling

1st (B♭), ♭3rd (D♭), 5th (F), 6th (G)

A#/Bb6sus4
6th Suspended 4th

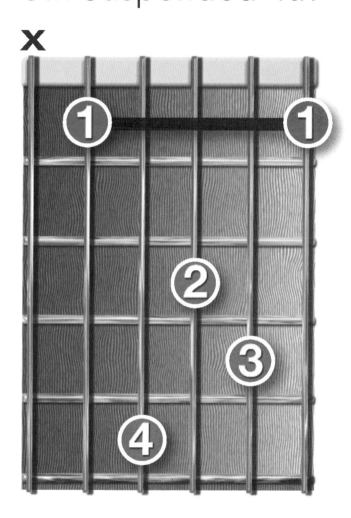

Chord Spelling
1st (Bb), 4th (Eb), 5th (F), 6th (G)

A

A#/Bb

B

C

C#/Db

D

D#/Eb

E

F

F#/Gb

G

G#/Ab

A#/B♭maj7
Major 7th

A#/B♭

B

C

C#/D♭

D

D#/E♭

E

F

F#/G♭

G

G#/A♭

X

Chord Spelling
1st (B♭), 3rd (D), 5th (F), 7th (A)

FREE ACCESS on smartphones
including iPhone & Android

Using any QR code app
scan and **HEAR** the chord

A#/B♭m7
Minor 7th

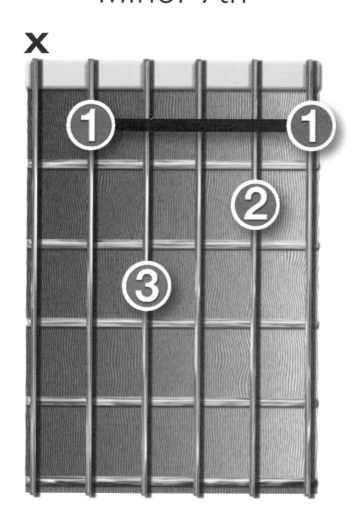

Chord Spelling
1st (B♭), ♭3rd (D♭), 5th (F), ♭7th (A♭)

FREE ACCESS on smartphones
including iPhone & Android

Using any QR code app
scan and **HEAR** the chord

A♯/B♭7
Dominant 7th

Chord Spelling
1st (B♭), 3rd (D), 5th (F), ♭7th (A♭)

A
A♯/B♭
B
C
C♯/D♭
D
D♯/E♭
E
F
F♯/G♭
G
G♯/A♭

A♯/B♭°7
Diminished 7th

Chord Spelling

1st (B♭), ♭3rd (D♭), ♭5th (F♭), ♭♭7th (A♭♭)

A
B
C
C♯/D♭
D
D♯/E♭
E
F
F♯/G♭
G
G♯/A♭

FREE ACCESS on smartphones
including iPhone & Android

Using any QR code app
scan and **HEAR** the chord

A♯/B♭7sus4
Dominant 7th Suspended 4th

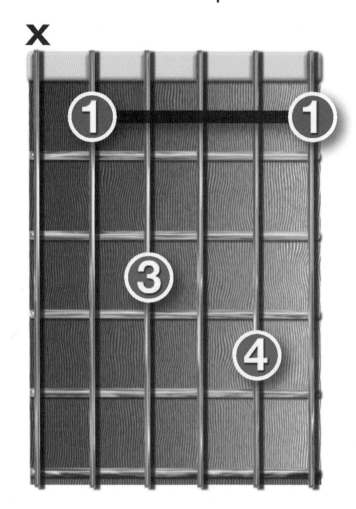

Chord Spelling
1st (B♭), 4th (E♭), 5th (F), ♭7th (A♭)

FREE ACCESS on smartphones
including iPhone & Android

Using any QR code app
scan and **HEAR** the chord

A
A♯/B♭
B
C
C♯/D♭
D
D♯/E♭
E
F
F♯/G♭
G
G♯/A♭

A#/B♭maj9
Major 9th

Chord Spelling
1st (B♭), 3rd (D), 5th (F), 7th (A), 9th (C)

FREE ACCESS on smartphones
including iPhone & Android

Using any QR code app
scan and **HEAR** the chord

A#/B♭m9
Minor 9th

X   X

4

① ② ③ ④

Chord Spelling
1st (B♭), ♭3rd (D♭), 5th (F), ♭7th (A♭), 9th (C)

A♯/B♭9
Dominant 9th

Chord Spelling
1st (B♭), 3rd (D), 5th (F), ♭7th (A♭), 9th (C)

A

A♯/B♭

B

C

C♯/D♭

D

D♯/E♭

E

F

F♯/G♭

G

G♯/A♭

A♯/B♭maj11
Major 11th

Chord Spelling
1st (B♭), 3rd (D), 5th (F), 7th (A), 9th (C), 11th (E♭)

A
A♯/B♭
B
C
C♯/D♭
D
D♯/E♭
E
F
F♯/G♭
G
G♯/A♭

A♯/B♭maj13
Major 13th

Chord Spelling
1st (B♭), 3rd (D), 5th (F), 7th (A), 9th (C), 11th (E♭), 13th (G)

B
Major

Chord Spelling
1st (B), 3rd (D#), 5th (F#)

FREE ACCESS on smartphones
including iPhone & Android

Using any QR code app
scan and **HEAR** the chord

Bm
Minor

X

Chord Spelling
1st (B), ♭3rd (D), 5th (F♯)

A

A♯/B♭

B

C

C♯/D♭

D

D♯/E♭

E

F

F♯/G♭

G

G♯/A♭

B+
Augmented Triad

Chord Spelling
1st (B), 3rd (D#), #5th (Fx)

A

A#/B♭

B

C

C#/D♭

D

D#/E♭

E

F

F#/G♭

G

G#/A♭

B°
Diminished Triad

Chord Spelling
1st (B), ♭3rd (D), ♭5th (F)

A

A#/B♭

B

C

C#/D♭

D

D#/E♭

E

F

F#/G♭

G

G#/A♭

Bsus2
Suspended 2nd

X

Chord Spelling
1st (B), 2nd (C#), 5th (F#)

Bsus4
Suspended 4th

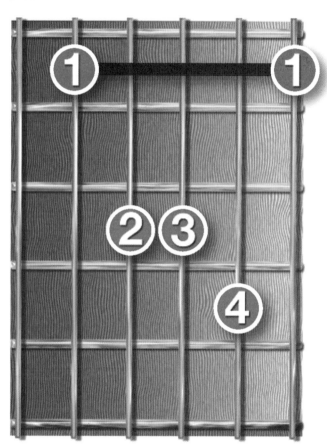

Chord Spelling
1st (B), 4th (E), 5th (F#)

A
A#/Bb
B
C
C#/Db
D
D#/Eb
E
F
F#/Gb
G
G#/Ab

B5
5th (Power Chord)

Chord Spelling
1st (B), 5th (F♯)

B6
Major 6th

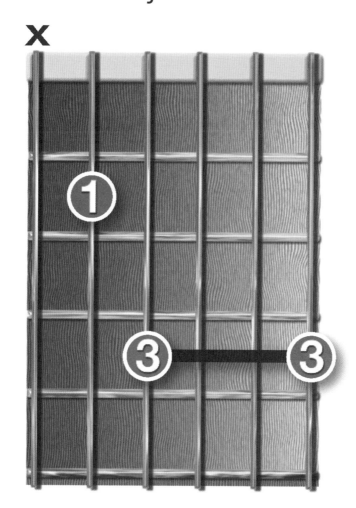

X

Chord Spelling
1st (B), 3rd (D♯), 5th (F♯), 6th (G♯)

Bm6
Minor 6th

Chord Spelling
1st (B), ♭3rd (D), 5th (F♯), 6th (G♯)

B6sus4
6th Suspended 4th

X   O

A
A#/Bb
B
C
C#/Db
D
D#/Eb
E
F
F#/Gb
G
G#/Ab

Chord Spelling
1st (B), 4th (E), 5th (F#), 6th (G#)

Bmaj7
Major 7th

A
A#/Bb
B
C
C#/Db
D
D#/Eb
E
F
F#/Gb
G
G#/Ab

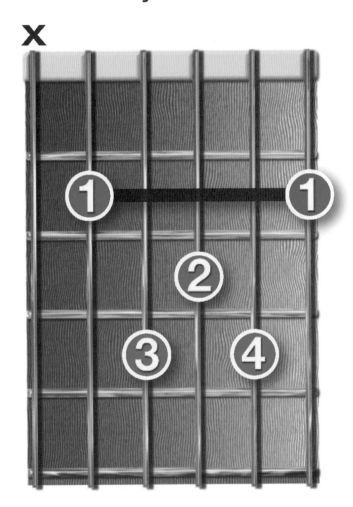

Chord Spelling
1st (B), 3rd (D#), 5th (F#), 7th (A#)

FREE ACCESS on smartphones
including iPhone & Android

Using any QR code app
scan and **HEAR** the chord

Bm7
Minor 7th

X

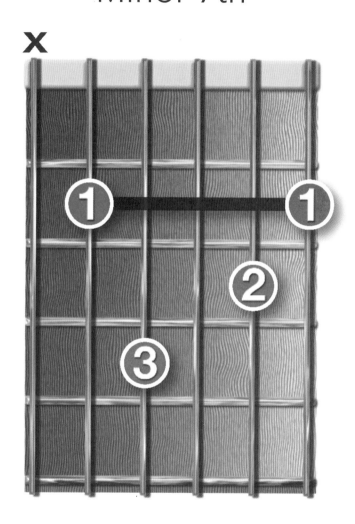

Chord Spelling
1st (B), ♭3rd (D), 5th (F♯), ♭7th (A)

A
A♯/B♭
B
C
C♯/D♭
D
D♯/E♭
E
F
F♯/G♭
G
G♯/A♭

B7
Dominant 7th

X

Chord Spelling
1st (B), 3rd (D#), 5th (F#), b7th (A)

B°7
Diminished 7th

A

A#/Bb

B

C

C#/Db

D

D#/Eb

E

F

F#/Gb

G

G#/Ab

Chord Spelling

1st (B), b3rd (D), b5th (F), bb7th (Ab)

FREE ACCESS on smartphones
including iPhone & Android

Using any QR code app
scan and **HEAR** the chord

B7sus4
Dominant 7th Suspended 4th

X   **O**

Chord Spelling
1st (B), 4th (E), 5th (F#), ♭7th (A)

A
A#/B♭
B
C
C#/D♭
D
D#/E♭
E
F
F#/G♭
G
G#/A♭

Bmaj9
Major 9th

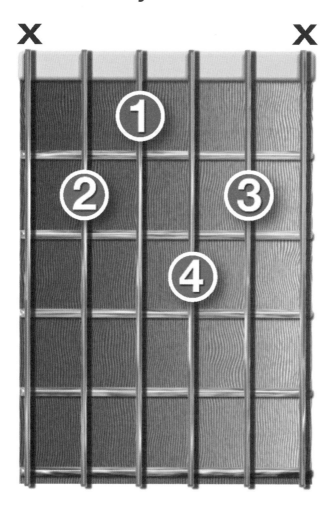

Chord Spelling

1st (B), 3rd (D♯), 5th (F♯), 7th (A♯), 9th (C♯)

Bm9
Minor 9th

Chord Spelling
1st (B), ♭3rd (D), 5th (F♯), ♭7th (A), 9th (C♯)

B9
Dominant 9th

Chord Spelling
1st (B), 3rd (D#), 5th (F#), b7th (A), 9th (C#)

FREE ACCESS on smartphones including iPhone & Android

Using any QR code app scan and **HEAR** the chord

Bmaj11
Major 11th

Chord Spelling
1st (B), 3rd (D♯), 5th (F♯), 7th (A♯), 9th (C♯), 11th (E)

Bmaj13
Major 13th

X

Chord Spelling
1st (B), 3rd (D#), 5th (F#), 7th (A#), 9th (C#), 11th (E), 13th (G#)

FREE ACCESS on smartphones including iPhone & Android

Using any QR code app scan and **HEAR** the chord

C
Major

Chord Spelling
1st (C), 3rd (E), 5th (G)

FREE ACCESS on smartphones
including iPhone & Android

Using any QR code app
scan and **HEAR** the chord

A

A#/B♭

B

C

C#/D♭

D

D#/E♭

E

F

F#/G♭

G

G#/A♭

Cm
Minor

3

Chord Spelling
1st (C), ♭3rd (E♭), 5th (G)

A

A#/B♭

B

C

C#/D♭

D

D#/E♭

E

F

F#/G♭

G

G#/A♭

C+
Augmented Triad

X   O

Chord Spelling

1st (C), 3rd (E), #5th (G#)

C°
Diminished Triad

X   X

3

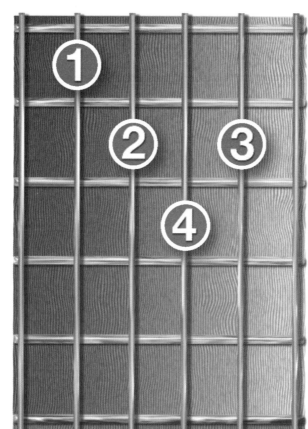

Chord Spelling
1st (C), ♭3rd (E♭), ♭5th (G♭)

A
A♯/B♭
B
C
C♯/D♭
D
D♯/E♭
E
F
F♯/G♭
G
G♯/A♭

Csus2
Suspended 2nd

X   O   O

Chord Spelling
1st (C), 2nd (D), 5th (G)

Csus4
Suspended 4th

X   **O**

Chord Spelling
1st (C), 4th (F), 5th (G)

A

A#/Bb

B

C

C#/Db

D

D#/Eb

E

F

F#/Gb

G

G#/Ab

C5
5th (Power Chord)

A

A#/Bb

B

C

C#/Db

D

D#/Eb

E

F

F#/Gb

G

G#/Ab

Chord Spelling
1st (C), 5th (G)

C6
Major 6th

X

3

Chord Spelling
1st (C), 3rd (E), 5th (G), 6th (A)

A
A#/Bb
B
C
C#/Db
D
D#/Eb
E
F
F#/Gb
G
G#/Ab

Cm6
Minor 6th

Chord Spelling
1st (C), ♭3rd (E♭), 5th (G), 6th (A)

C6sus4
6th Suspended 4th

Chord Spelling
1st (C), 4th (F), 5th (G), 6th (A)

Cmaj7
Major 7th

Chord Spelling
1st (C), 3rd (E), 5th (G), 7th (B)

Cm7
Minor 7th

X

3

A
A#/Bb
B
C
C#/Db
D
D#/Eb
E
F
F#/Gb
G
G#/Ab

Chord Spelling
1st (C), ♭3rd (E♭), 5th (G), ♭7th (B♭)

C7
Dominant 7th

Chord Spelling
1st (C), 3rd (E), 5th (G), ♭7th (B♭)

A

A♯/B♭

B

C

C♯/D♭

D

D♯/E♭

E

F

F♯/G♭

G

G♯/A♭

C°7
Diminished 7th

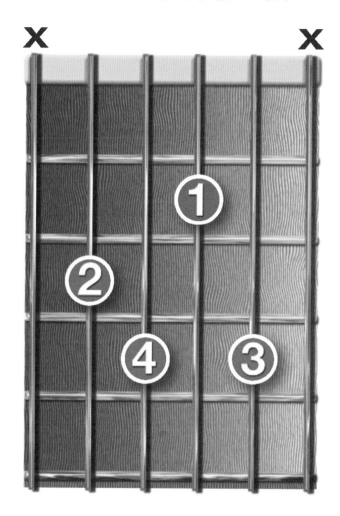

Chord Spelling
1st (C), ♭3rd (E♭), ♭5th (G♭), ♭♭7th (B♭♭)

A
A♯/B♭
B
C
C♯/D♭
D
D♯/E♭
E
F
F♯/G♭
G
G♯/A♭

C7sus4
Dominant 7th Suspended 4th

X   X

3

① ② ③ ④

Chord Spelling
1st (C), 4th (F), 5th (G), ♭7th (B♭)

A
A♯/B♭
B
C
C♯/D♭
D
D♯/E♭
E
F
F♯/G♭
G
G♯/A♭

Cmaj9
Major 9th

Chord Spelling
1st (C), 3rd (E), 5th (G), 7th (B), 9th (D)

FREE ACCESS on smartphones
including iPhone & Android

Using any QR code app
scan and **HEAR** the chord

A

A#/Bb

B

C

C#/Db

D

D#/Eb

E

F

F#/Gb

G

G#/Ab

Cm9
Minor 9th

X X

A

A#/Bb

B

C

C#/Db

D

D#/Eb

E

F

F#/Gb

G

G#/Ab

6

① ② ③ ④

Chord Spelling
1st (C), b3rd (Eb), 5th (G), b7th (Bb), 9th (D)

C9
Dominant 9th

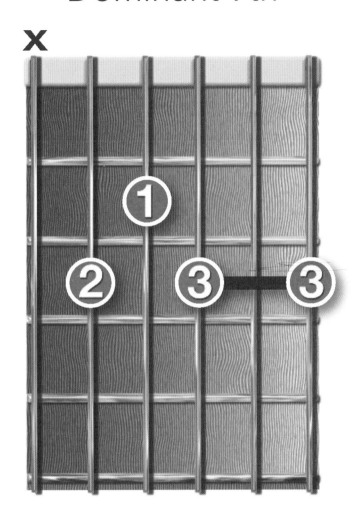

Chord Spelling
1st (C), 3rd (E), 5th (G), ♭7th (B♭), 9th (D)

FREE ACCESS on smartphones including iPhone & Android

Using any QR code app scan and **HEAR** the chord

Cmaj11
Major 11th

Chord Spelling
1st (C), 3rd (E), 5th (G), 7th (B), 9th (D), 11th (F)

Cmaj13
Major 13th

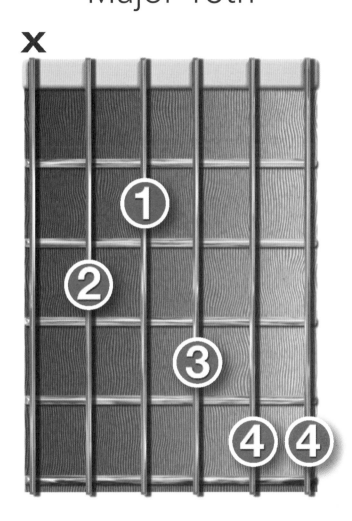

X

Chord Spelling
1st (C), 3rd (E), 5th (G), 7th (B), 9th (D), 11th (F), 13th (A)

A

A#/Bb

B

C

C#/Db

D

D#/Eb

E

F

F#/Gb

G

G#/Ab

C#/Db
Major

X

Chord Spelling
1st (C#), 3rd (E#), 5th (G#)

A

A#/Bb

B

C

C#/Db

D

D#/Eb

E

F

F#/Gb

G

Ab/G#

C#/D♭m
Minor

X

4

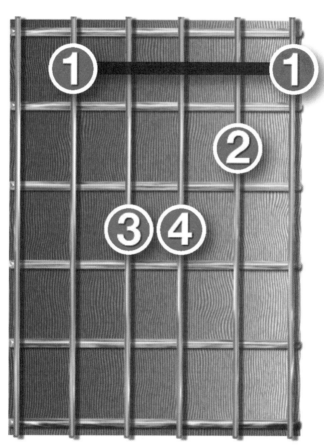

Chord Spelling
1st (C#), ♭3rd (E), 5th (G#)

C#/D♭+
Augmented Triad

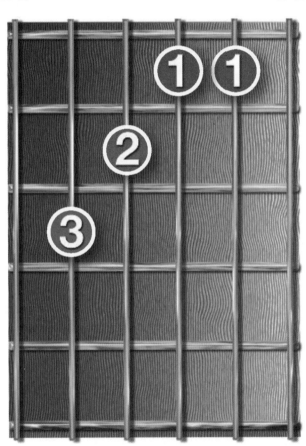

X   **X**

2

Chord Spelling
1st (C#), 3rd (E#), #5th (Gx)

A
A#/B♭
B
C
C#/D♭
D
D#/E♭
E
F
F#/G♭
G
A♭/G#

C♯/D♭°
Diminished Triad

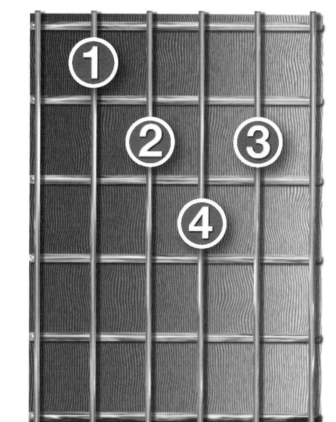

X   O

4

① ② ③ ④

A
A♯/B♭
B
C
C♯/D♭
D
D♯/E♭
E
F
F♯/G♭
G
A♭/G♯

Chord Spelling
1st (C♯), ♭3rd (E), ♭5th (G)

C#/D♭sus2
Suspended 2nd

Chord Spelling
1st (C#), 2nd (D#), 5th (G#)

A

A#/B♭

B

C

C#/D♭

D

D#/E♭

E

F

F#/G♭

G

G#/A♭

C#/D♭sus4
Suspended 4th

X

4

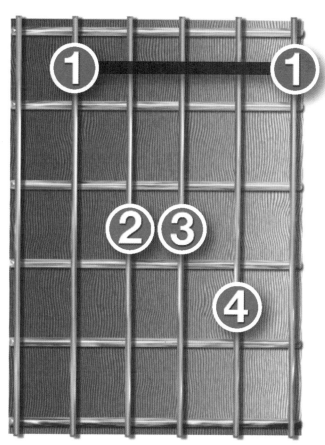

Chord Spelling
1st (C#), 4th (F#), 5th (G#)

A

A#/B♭

B

C

C#/D♭

D

D#/E♭

E

F

F#/G♭

G

G#/A♭

C#/D♭5

5th (Power Chord)

X   X   X

4

Chord Spelling

1st (C#), 5th (G#)

C#/Db6
Major 6th

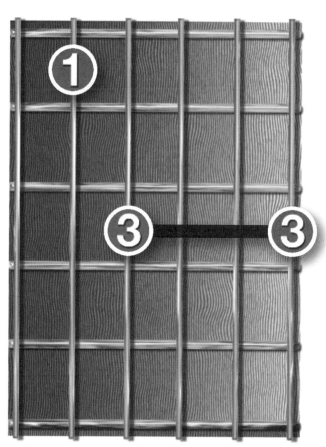

Chord Spelling
1st (C#), 3rd (E#), 5th (G#), 6th (A#)

A
A#/Bb
B
C
C#/Db
D
D#/Eb
E
F
F#/Gb
G
Ab/G#

C#/D♭m6
Minor 6th

Chord Spelling
1st (C#), ♭3rd (E), 5th (G#), 6th (A#)

FREE ACCESS on smartphones
including iPhone & Android

Using any QR code app
scan and **HEAR** the chord

Sidebar: A, A#/B♭, B, C, **C#/D♭**, D, D#/E♭, E, F, F#/G♭, G, A♭/G#

C♯/D♭6sus4
6th Suspended 4th

Chord Spelling
1st (C♯), 4th (F♯), 5th (G♯), 6th (A♯)

C#/D♭maj7
Major 7th

A

A#/B♭

B

C

C#/D♭

D

D#/E♭

E

F

F#/G♭

G

A♭/G#

Chord Spelling
1st (C#), 3rd (E#), 5th (G#), 7th (B#)

C#/D♭m7
Minor 7th

X

2

Chord Spelling
1st (C#), ♭3rd (E), 5th (G#), ♭7th (B)

FREE ACCESS on smartphones
including iPhone & Android

Using any QR code app
scan and **HEAR** the chord

C#/D♭7
Dominant 7th

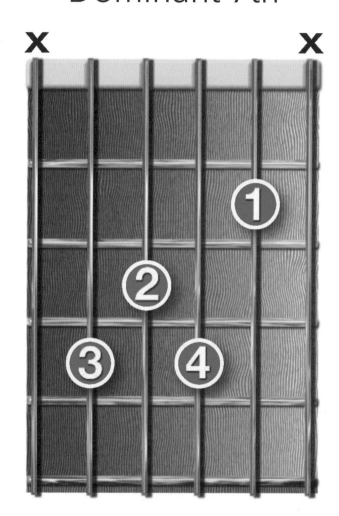

Chord Spelling
1st (C#), 3rd (E#), 5th (G#), ♭7th (B)

C#/D♭°7
Diminished 7th

X

3

Chord Spelling
1st (C#), ♭3rd (E), ♭5th (G), ♭♭7th (B♭)

C#/Db7sus4
Dominant 7th Suspended 4th

4

X   X

① ② ③   ④

Chord Spelling
1st (C#), 4th (F#), 5th (G#), b7th (B)

C#/D♭maj9
Major 9th

X   **X**

3

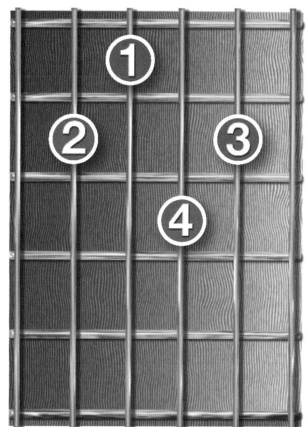

Chord Spelling
1st (C#), 3rd (E#), 5th (G#), 7th (B#), 9th (D#)

A
A#/B♭
B
C
C#/D♭
D
D#/E♭
E
F
F#/G♭
G
A♭/G#

C#/D♭m9
Minor 9th

Chord Spelling
1st (C#), ♭3rd (E), 5th (G#), ♭7th (B), 9th (D#)

C#/Db9

Dominant 9th

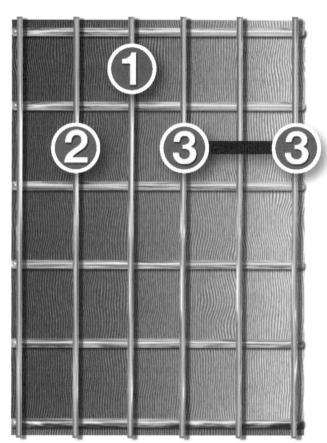

X

3

A

A#/Bb

B

C

C#/Db

D

Db/Eb

E

F

F#/Gb

G

Ab/G#

Chord Spelling

1st (C#), 3rd (E#), 5th (G#), b7th (B), 9th (D#)

C#/D♭maj11
Major 11th

X

Chord Spelling
1st (C#), 3rd (E#), 5th (G#), 7th (B#), 9th (D#), 11th (F#)

A

A#/B♭

B

C

C#/D♭

D

D#/E♭

E

F

F#/G♭

G

A♭/G#

C#/D♭maj13
Major 13th

X

3

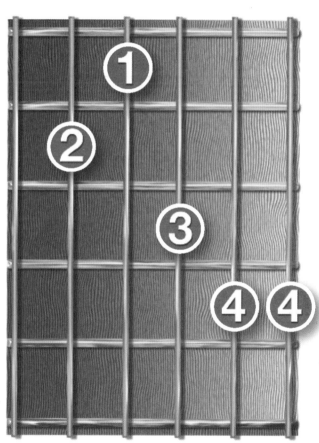

Chord Spelling
1st (C#), 3rd (E#), 5th (G#), 7th (B#), 9th (D#), 11th (F#), 13th (A#)

FREE ACCESS on smartphones
including iPhone & Android

Using any QR code app
scan and **HEAR** the chord

A

A#/B♭

B

C

C#/D♭

D

D#/E♭

E

F

F#/G♭

G

A♭/G#

D
Major

A
A#/Bb
B
C
C#/Db
D
D#/Eb
E
F
F#/Gb
G
G#/Ab

Chord Spelling
1st (D), 3rd (F#), 5th (A)

Dm
Minor

X X O

Chord Spelling
1st (D), ♭3rd (F), 5th (A)

D+
Augmented Triad

3

Chord Spelling
1st (D), 3rd (F#), #5th (A#)

FREE ACCESS on smartphones
including iPhone & Android

Using any QR code app
scan and **HEAR** the chord

D°
Diminished Triad

X X O

Chord Spelling
1st (D), ♭3rd (F), ♭5th (A♭)

A
A♯/B♭
B
C
C♯/D♭
D
D♯/E♭
E
F
F♯/G♭
G
G♯/A♭

FREE ACCESS on smartphones including iPhone & Android

Using any QR code app scan and **HEAR** the chord

Dsus2
Suspended 2nd

A
A#/Bb
B
C
C#/Db
D
D#/Eb
E
F
F#/Gb
G
G#/Ab

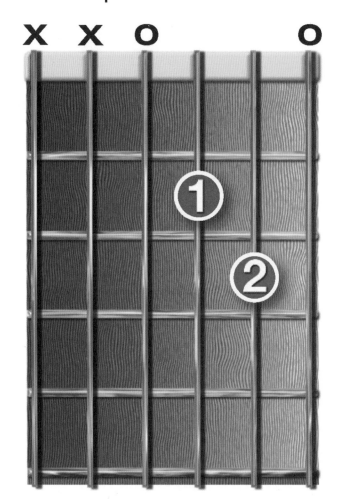

Chord Spelling
1st (D), 2nd (E), 5th (A)

Dsus4
Suspended 4th

Chord Spelling
1st (D), 4th (G), 5th (A)

D5
5th (Power Chord)

Chord Spelling
1st (D), 5th (A)

D6
Major 6th

Chord Spelling

1st (D), 3rd (F♯), 5th (A), 6th (B)

A

A♯/B♭

B

C

C♯/D♭

D

D♯/E♭

E

F

F♯/G♭

G

G♯/A♭

Dm6
Minor 6th

Chord Spelling
1st (D), ♭3rd (F), 5th (A), 6th (B)

D6sus4
6th Suspended 4th

Chord Spelling
1st (D), 4th (G), 5th (A), 6th (B)

Dmaj7
Major 7th

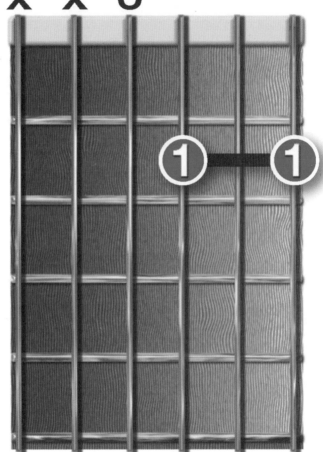

Chord Spelling
1st (D), 3rd (F#), 5th (A), 7th (C#)

Dm7
Minor 7th

Chord Spelling
1st (D), ♭3rd (F), 5th (A), ♭7th (C)

A

A#/B♭

B

C

C#/D♭

D

D#/E♭

E

F

F#/G♭

G

G#/A♭

D7
Dominant 7th

X   X   O

Chord Spelling
1st (D), 3rd (F#), 5th (A), ♭7th (C)

A

A#/B♭

B

C

C#/D♭

D

D#/E♭

E

F

F#/G♭

G

G#/A♭

D°7
Diminished 7th

X   X   O   O

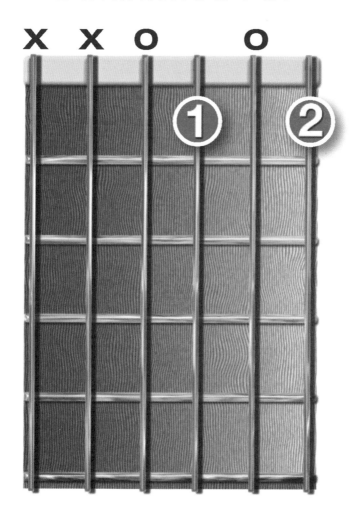

Chord Spelling
1st (D), ♭3rd (F), ♭5th (A♭), ♭♭7th (B)

A
A♯/B♭
B
C
C♯/D♭
D
D♯/E♭
E
F
F♯/G♭
G
G♯/A♭

D7sus4
Dominant 7th Suspended 4th

Chord Spelling
1st (D), 4th (G), 5th (A), ♭7th (C)

A

A#/B♭

B

C

C#/D♭

D

D#/E♭

E

F

F#/G♭

G

G#/A♭

Dmaj9
Major 9th

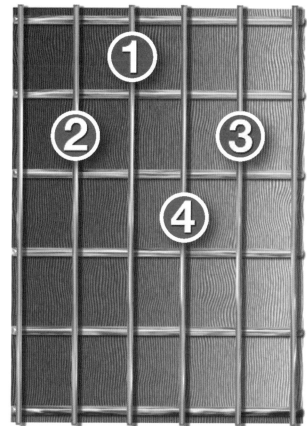

X   **X**

4

Chord Spelling
1st (D), 3rd (F♯), 5th (A), 7th (C♯), 9th (E)

A

A♯/B♭

B

C

C♯/D♭

D

D♯/E♭

E

F

F♯/G♭

G

G♯/A♭

Dm9
Minor 9th

Chord Spelling
1st (D), ♭3rd (F), 5th (A), ♭7th (C), 9th (E)

D9
Dominant 9th

X

4

Chord Spelling
1st (D), 3rd (F#), 5th (A), ♭7th (C), 9th (E)

FREE ACCESS on smartphones including iPhone & Android

Using any QR code app scan and **HEAR** the chord

Dmaj11
Major 11th

X X O O

② ③

Chord Spelling

1st (D), 3rd (F♯), 5th (A), 7th (C♯), 9th (E), 11th (G)

Dmaj13
Major 13th

X

4

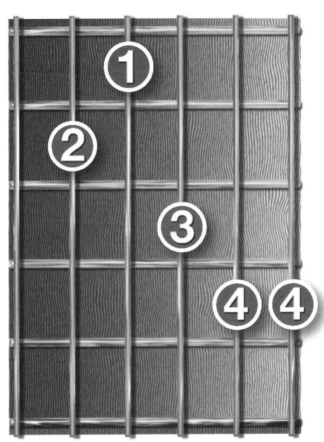

Chord Spelling
1st (D), 3rd (F#), 5th (A), 7th (C#), 9th (E), 11th (G), 13th (B)

FREE ACCESS on smartphones
including iPhone & Android

Using any QR code app
scan and **HEAR** the chord

D♯/E♭
Major

X

3

Chord Spelling
1st (E♭), 3rd (G), 5th (B♭)

D#/E♭m
Minor

Chord Spelling
1st (E♭), ♭3rd (G♭), 5th (B♭)

A

A#/B♭

B

C

C#/D♭

D

D#/E♭

E

F

F#/G♭

G

G#/A♭

D#/E♭+

Augmented Triad

Chord Spelling

1st (E♭), 3rd (G), #5th (B)

A
A#/B♭
B
C
C#/D♭
D
D#/E♭
E
F
F#/G♭
G
G#/A♭

D#/Eb°
Diminished Triad

Chord Spelling
1st (Eb), b3rd (Gb), b5th (Bbb)

A

A#/Bb

B

C

C#/Db

D

D#/Eb

E

F

F#/Gb

G

G#/Ab

D♯/E♭sus2
Suspended 2nd

Chord Spelling
1st (E♭), 2nd (F), 5th (B♭)

D#/E♭sus4
Suspended 4th

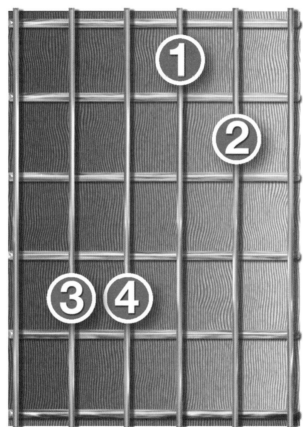

Chord Spelling
1st (E♭), 4th (A♭), 5th (B♭)

A

A#/B♭

B

C

C#/D♭

D

D#/E♭

E

F

F#/G♭

G

G#/A♭

FREE ACCESS on smartphones including iPhone & Android

Using any QR code app scan and **HEAR** the chord

D♯/E♭5
5th (Power Chord)

A
A♯/B♭
B
C
C♯/D♭
D
D♯/E♭
E
F
F♯/G♭
G
G♯/A♭

Chord Spelling
1st (E♭), 5th (B♭)

D♯/E♭6
Major 6th

X   X

① ①

③ ④

Chord Spelling
1st (E♭), 3rd (G), 5th (B♭), 6th (C)

A
A♯/B♭
B
C
C♯/D♭
D
D♯/E♭
E
F
F♯/G♭
G
G♯/A♭

D#/E♭m6
Minor 6th

X

4

Chord Spelling
1st (E♭), ♭3rd (G♭), 5th (B♭), 6th (C)

D#/E♭6sus4
6th Suspended 4th

Chord Spelling
1st (E♭), 4th (A♭), 5th (B♭), 6th (C)

D#/E♭maj7
Major 7th

X

3

Chord Spelling
1st (E♭), 3rd (G), 5th (B♭), 7th (D)

A

A#/B♭

B

C

C#/D♭

D

D#/E♭

E

F

F#/G♭

G

G#/A♭

D#/E♭m7
Minor 7th

X

4

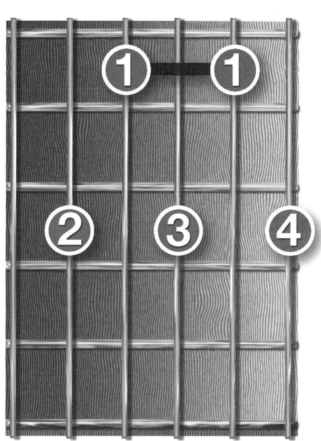

Chord Spelling
1st (E♭), ♭3rd (G♭), 5th (B♭), ♭7th (D♭)

A

A#/B♭

B

C

C#/D♭

D

D#/E♭

E

F

F#/G♭

G

G#/A♭

D♯/E♭7
Dominant 7th

Chord Spelling
1st (E♭), 3rd (G), 5th (B♭), ♭7th (D♭)

FREE ACCESS on smartphones
including iPhone & Android

Using any QR code app
scan and **HEAR** the chord

D♯/E♭°7
Diminished 7th

Chord Spelling
1st (E♭), ♭3rd (G♭), ♭5th (B♭♭), ♭♭7th (D♭♭)

A

A♯/B♭

B

C

C♯/D♭

D

D♯/E♭

E

F

F♯/G♭

G

G♯/A♭

D♯/E♭7sus4
Dominant 7th Suspended 4th

A
A♯/B♭
B
C
C♯/D♭
D
D♯/E♭
E
F
F♯/G♭
G
G♯/A♭

Chord Spelling
1st (E♭), 4th (A♭), 5th (B♭), ♭7th (D♭)

D♯/E♭maj9
Major 9th

X   X

5

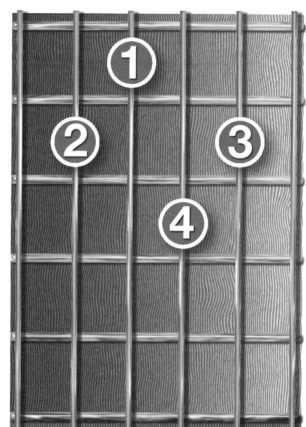

Chord Spelling

1st (E♭), 3rd (G), 5th (B♭), 7th (D), 9th (F)

A
A♯/B♭
B
C
C♯/D♭
D
D♯/E♭
E
F
F♯/G♭
G
G♯/A♭

D#/E♭m9
Minor 9th

Chord Spelling
1st (E♭), ♭3rd (G♭), 5th (B♭), ♭7th (D♭), 9th (F)

D♯/E♭9
Dominant 9th

Chord Spelling
1st (E♭), 3rd (G), 5th (B♭), ♭7th (D♭), 9th (F)

A

A♯/B♭

B

C

C♯/D♭

D

D♯/E♭

E

F

F♯/G♭

G

G♯/A♭

FREE ACCESS on smartphones
including iPhone & Android

Using any QR code app
scan and **HEAR** the chord

D#/E♭maj11
Major 11th

Chord Spelling
1st (E♭), 3rd (G), 5th (B♭), 7th (D), 9th (F), 11th (A♭)

D♯/E♭maj13
Major 13th

X

5

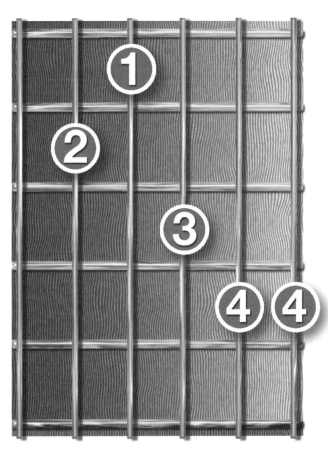

A

A♯/B♭

B

C

C♯/D♭

D

D♯/E♭

E

F

F♯/G♭

G

G♯/A♭

Chord Spelling

1st (E♭), 3rd (G), 5th (B♭), 7th (D), 9th (F), 11th (A♭), 13th (C)

E
Major

Chord Spelling
1st (E), 3rd (G#), 5th (B)

FREE ACCESS on smartphones
including iPhone & Android

Using any QR code app
scan and **HEAR** the chord

Em
Minor

Chord Spelling
1st (E), ♭3rd (G), 5th (B)

A
A#/B♭
B
C
C#/D♭
D
D#/E♭
E
F
F#/G♭
G
G#/A♭

E+
Augmented Triad

Chord Spelling

1st (E), 3rd (G#), #5th (B#)

E°
Diminished Triad

Chord Spelling
1st (E), ♭3rd (G), ♭5th (B♭)

A

A♯/B♭

B

C

C♯/D♭

D

D♯/E♭

E

F

F♯/G♭

G

G♯/A♭

Esus2
Suspended 2nd

X   X

Chord Spelling
1st (E), 2nd (F♯), 5th (B)

Esus4
Suspended 4th

Chord Spelling
1st (E), 4th (A), 5th (B)

A
A#/B♭
B
C
C#/D♭
D
D#/E♭
E
F
F#/G♭
G
G#/A♭

FREE ACCESS on smartphones including iPhone & Android

Using any QR code app scan and **HEAR** the chord

E5
5th (Power Chord)

Chord Spelling
1st (E), 5th (B)

A

A♯/B♭

B

C

C♯/D♭

D

D♯/E♭

E

F

F♯/G♭

G

G♯/A♭

E6
Major 6th

Chord Spelling
1st (E), 3rd (G♯), 5th (B), 6th (C♯)

A
A♯/B♭
B
C
C♯/D♭
D
D♯/E♭
E
F
F♯/G♭
G
G♯/A♭

Em6
Minor 6th

O   O   O

②③   ④

Chord Spelling
1st (E), ♭3rd (G), 5th (B), 6th (C♯)

A

A♯/B♭

B

C

C♯/D♭

D

D♯/E♭

E

F

F♯/G♭

G

G♯/A♭

E6sus4
6th Suspended 4th

Chord Spelling
1st (E), 4th (A), 5th (B), 6th (C#)

Emaj7
Major 7th

O   O O

① ②

③

Chord Spelling
1st (E), 3rd (G#), 5th (B), 7th (D#)

Em7
Minor 7th

Chord Spelling
1st (E), ♭3rd (G), 5th (B), ♭7th (D)

A
A♯/B♭
B
C
C♯/D♭
D
D♯/E♭
E
F
F♯/G♭
G
G♯/A♭

FREE ACCESS on smartphones including iPhone & Android

Using any QR code app scan and **HEAR** the chord

E7
Dominant 7th

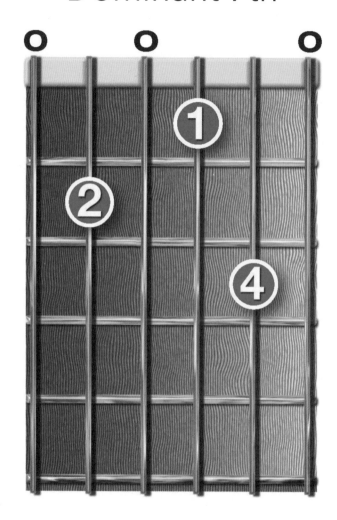

Chord Spelling
1st (E), 3rd (G♯), 5th (B), ♭7th (D)

E°7
Diminished 7th

Chord Spelling
1st (E), ♭3rd (G), ♭5th (B♭), ♭♭7th (D♭)

E7sus4
Dominant 7th Suspended 4th

Chord Spelling
1st (E), 4th (A), 5th (B), ♭7th (D)

Emaj9
Major 9th

Chord Spelling
1st (E), 3rd (G#), 5th (B), 7th (D#), 9th (F#)

A
A#/B♭
B
C
C#/D♭
D
D#/E♭
E
F
F#/G♭
G
G#/A♭

FREE ACCESS on smartphones including iPhone & Android

Using any QR code app scan and **HEAR** the chord

Em9

Minor 9th

Chord Spelling

1st (E), ♭3rd (G), 5th (B), ♭7th (D), 9th (F♯)

A
A♯/B♭
B
C
C♯/D♭
D
D♯/E♭
E
F
F♯/G♭
G
G♯/A♭

E9

Dominant 9th

Chord Spelling

1st (E), 3rd (G#), 5th (B), ♭7th (D), 9th (F#)

FREE ACCESS on smartphones
including iPhone & Android

Using any QR code app
scan and **HEAR** the chord

Emaj11
Major 11th

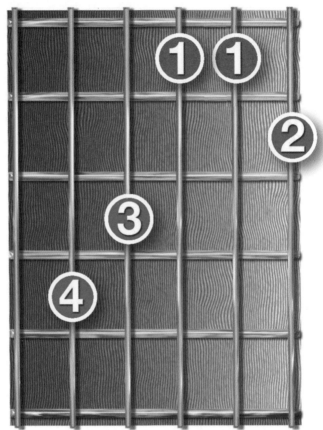

X

4

A
A#/Bb
B
C
C#/Db
D
D#/Eb
E
F
F#/Gb
G
G#/Ab

Chord Spelling
1st (E), 3rd (G#), 5th (B), 7th (D#), 9th (F#), 11th (A)

Emaj13
Major 13th

A
A#/Bb
B
C
C#/Db
D
D#/Eb
E
F
F#/Gb
G
G#/Ab

Chord Spelling
1st (E), 3rd (G#), 5th (B), 7th (D#), 9th (F), 11th (A), 13th (C#)

F
Major

Chord Spelling
1st (F), 3rd (A), 5th (C)

Fm
Minor

A

A#/Bb

B

C

C#/Db

D

D#/Eb

E

F

F#/Gb

G

G#/Ab

Chord Spelling
1st (F), b3rd (Ab), 5th (C)

F+
Augmented Triad

Chord Spelling
1st (F), 3rd (A), ♯5th (C♯)

A

A♯/B♭

B

C

C♯/D♭

D

D♯/E♭

E

F

F♯/G♭

G

G♯/A♭

F°
Diminished Triad

Chord Spelling
1st (F), ♭3rd (A♭), ♭5th (C♭)

A
A#/B♭
B
C
C#/D♭
D
D#/E♭
E
F
F#/G♭
G
G#/A♭

Fsus2
Suspended 2nd

Chord Spelling
1st (F), 2nd (G), 5th (C)

A
A#/Bb
B
C
C#/Db
D
D#/Eb
E
F
F#/Gb
G
G#/Ab

Fsus4
Suspended 4th

A

A#/Bb

B

C

C#/Db

D

D#/Eb

E

F

F#/Gb

G

G#/Ab

Chord Spelling
1st (F), 4th (Bb), 5th (C)

F5
5th (Power Chord)

X X X

① ③ ④

Chord Spelling
1st (F), 5th (C)

A
A#/Bb
B
C
C#/Db
D
D#/Eb
E
F
F#/Gb
G
G#/Ab

F6
Major 6th

Chord Spelling
1st (F), 3rd (A), 5th (C), 6th (D)

A

A#/Bb

B

C

C#/Db

D

D#/Eb

E

F

F#/Gb

G

G#/Ab

Fm6
Minor 6th

A

A#/Bb

B

C

C#/Db

D

D#/Eb

E

F

F#/Gb

G

G#/Ab

Chord Spelling

1st (F), b3rd (Ab), 5th (C), 6th (D)

F6sus4
6th Suspended 4th

Chord Spelling
1st (F), 4th (B♭), 5th (C), 6th (D)

185

A

A♯/B♭

B

C

C♯/D♭

D

D♯/E♭

E

F

F♯/G♭

G

G♯/A♭

Fmaj7
Major 7th

Chord Spelling
1st (F), 3rd (A), 5th (C), 7th (E)

A

A#/B♭

B

C

C#/D♭

D

D#/E♭

E

F

F#/G♭

G

G#/A♭

Fm7
Minor 7th

Chord Spelling

1st (F), ♭3rd (A♭), 5th (C), ♭7th (E♭)

FREE ACCESS on smartphones
including iPhone & Android

Using any QR code app
scan and **HEAR** the chord

A

A#/B♭

B

C

C#/D♭

D

D#/E♭

E

F

F#/G♭

G

G#/A♭

F7
Dominant 7th

Chord Spelling
1st (F), 3rd (A), 5th (C), ♭7th (E♭)

A

A♯/B♭

B

C

C♯/D♭

D

D♯/E♭

E

F

F♯/G♭

G

G♯/A♭

F°7
Diminished 7th

X   X

3

① ② ③ ④

A
A#/Bb
B
C
C#/Db
D
D#/Eb
E
F
F#/Gb
G
G#/Ab

Chord Spelling
1st (F), b3rd (Ab), b5th (Cb), bb7th (Ebb)

F7sus4
Dominant 7th Suspended 4th

Chord Spelling
1st (F), 4th (B♭), 5th (C), ♭7th (E♭)

A

A#/B♭

B

C

C#/D♭

D

D#/E♭

E

F

F#/G♭

G

G#/A♭

Fmaj9
Major 9th

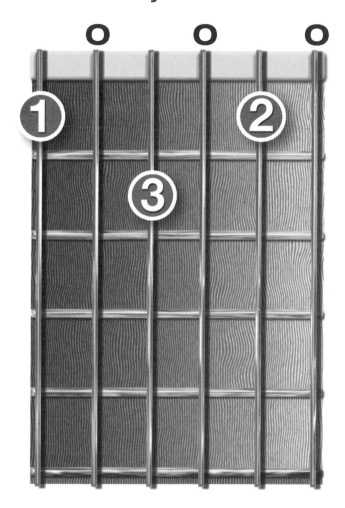

Chord Spelling
1st (F), 3rd (A), 5th (C), 7th (E), 9th (G)

Fm9
Minor 9th

A
A♯/B♭
B
C
C♯/D♭
D
D♯/E♭
E
F
F♯/G♭
G
G♯/A♭

Chord Spelling
1st (F), ♭3rd (A♭), 5th (C), ♭7th (E♭), 9th (G)

FREE ACCESS on smartphones including iPhone & Android

Using any QR code app scan and **HEAR** the chord

F9
Dominant 9th

Chord Spelling
1st (F), 3rd (A), 5th (C), ♭7th (E♭), 9th (G)

A

A♯/B♭

B

C

C♯/D♭

D

D♯/E♭

E

F

F♯/G♭

G

G♯/A♭

Fmaj11
Major 11th

Chord Spelling
1st (F), 3rd (A), 5th (C), 7th (E), 9th (G), 11th (B♭)

A

A#/B♭

B

C

C#/D♭

D

D#/E♭

E

F

F#/G♭

G

G#/A♭

FREE ACCESS on smartphones
including iPhone & Android

Using any QR code app
scan and **HEAR** the chord

Fmaj13
Major 13th

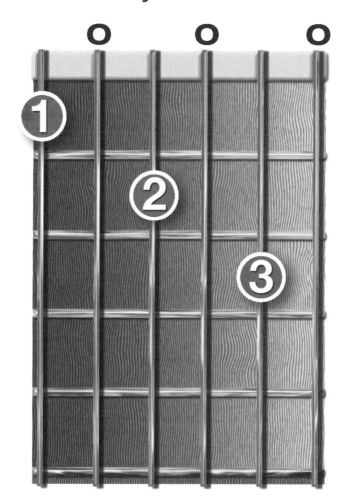

Chord Spelling
1st (F), 3rd (A), 5th (C), 7th (E), 9th (G), 11th (B♭), 13th (D)

A

A♯/B♭

B

C

C♯/D♭

D

D♯/E♭

E

F

F♯/G♭

G

G♯/A♭

F♯/G♭
Major

Chord Spelling
1st (F♯), 3rd (A♯), 5th (C♯)

F♯/G♭m
Minor

Chord Spelling
1st (F♯), ♭3rd (A), 5th (C♯)

A

A♯/B♭

B

C

C♯/D♭

D

D♯/E♭

E

F

F♯/G♭

G

G♯/A♭

F♯/G♭+
Augmented Triad

A
A♯/B♭
B
C
C♯/D♭
D
D♯/E♭
E
F
F♯/G♭
G
G♯/A♭

Chord Spelling
1st (F♯), 3rd (A♯), ♯5th (Cx)

F#/G♭°
Diminished Triad

X X

A

A#/B♭

B

C

C#/D♭

D

D#/E♭

E

F

F#/G♭

G

G#/A♭

Chord Spelling
1st (F#), ♭3rd (A), ♭5th (C)

F#/G♭sus2
Suspended 2nd

Chord Spelling
1st (F#), 2nd (G#), 5th (A#)

F♯/G♭sus4
Suspended 4th

Chord Spelling
1st (F♯), 4th (B), 5th (C♯)

A

A♯/B♭

B

C

C♯/D♭

D

D♯/E♭

E

F

F♯/G♭

G

G♯/A♭

F♯/G♭5

5th (Power Chord)

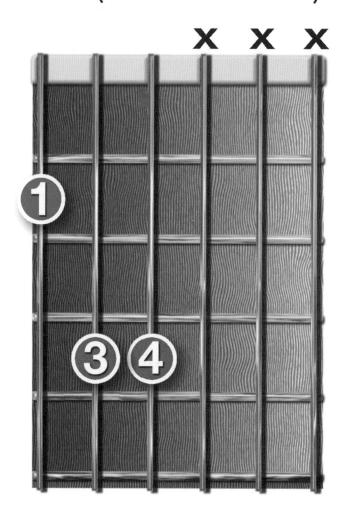

Chord Spelling

1st (F♯), 5th (C♯)

F♯/G♭6
Major 6th

X

A
A♯/B♭
B
C
C♯/D♭
D
D♯/E♭
E
F
F♯/G♭
G
G♯/A♭

Chord Spelling
1st (F♯), 3rd (A♯), 5th (C♯), 6th (D♯)

F#/G♭m6
Minor 6th

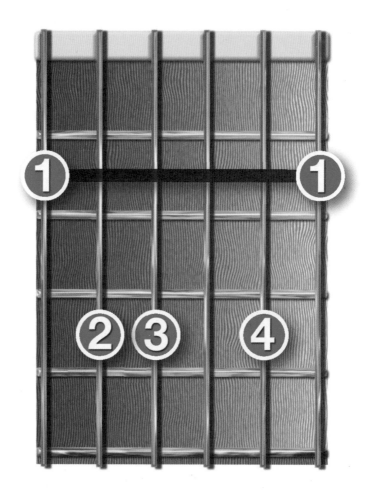

Chord Spelling
1st (F#), ♭3rd (A), 5th (C#), 6th (D#)

A

A#/B♭

B

C

C#/D♭

D

D#/E♭

E

F

F#/G♭

G

G#/A♭

F#/G♭6sus4
6th Suspended 4th

Chord Spelling
1st (F#), 4th (B), 5th (C#), 6th (D#)

A

A#/B♭

B

C

C#/D♭

D

D#/E♭

E

F

F#/G♭

G

G#/A♭

F#/G♭maj7
Major 7th

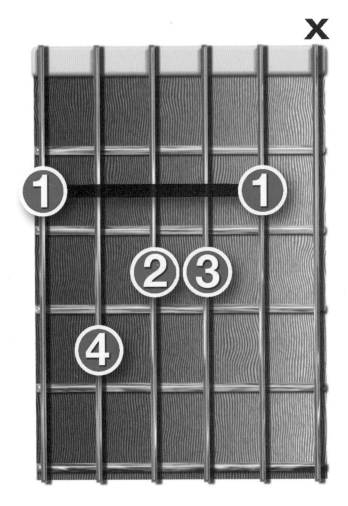

Chord Spelling
1st (F#), 3rd (A#), 5th (C#), 7th (F)

FREE ACCESS on smartphones
including iPhone & Android

Using any QR code app
scan and **HEAR** the chord

206

F♯/G♭m7
Minor 7th

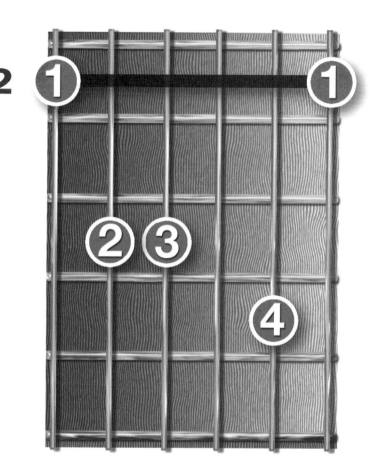

Chord Spelling
1st (F♯), ♭3rd (A), 5th (C♯), ♭7th (E)

FREE ACCESS on smartphones
including iPhone & Android

Using any QR code app
scan and **HEAR** the chord

F♯/G♭7
Dominant 7th

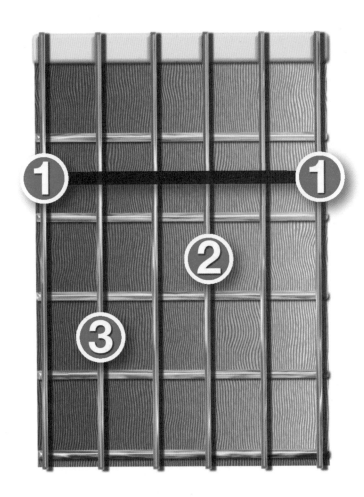

Chord Spelling
1st (F♯), 3rd (A♯), 5th (C♯), ♭7th (E)

F♯/G♭°7
Diminished 7th

X X

4

Chord Spelling
1st (F♯), ♭3rd (A), ♭5th (C), ♭♭7th (E♭)

A

A♯/B♭

B

C

C♯/D♭

D

D♯/E♭

E

F

F♯/G♭

G

G♯/A♭

F♯/G♭7sus4
Dominant 7th Suspended 4th

Chord Spelling
1st (F♯), 4th (B), 5th (C♯), ♭7th (E)

FREE ACCESS on smartphones
including iPhone & Android

Using any QR code app
scan and **HEAR** the chord

F#/G♭maj9
Major 9th

X

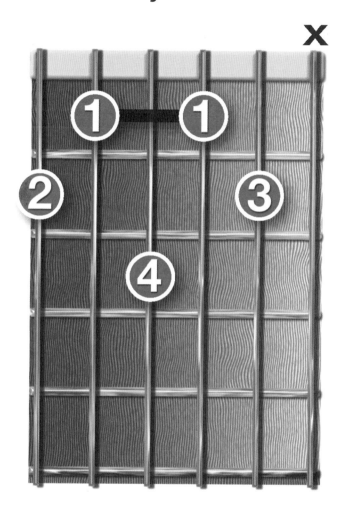

Chord Spelling
1st (F#), 3rd (A#), 5th (C#), 7th (E#), 9th (G#)

A

A#/B♭

B

C

C#/D♭

D

D#/E♭

E

F

F#/G♭

G

G#/A♭

F#/G♭m9
Minor 9th

A

A♯/B♭

B

C

C♯/D♭

D

D♯/E♭

E

F

F♯/G♭

G

G♯/A♭

Chord Spelling
1st (F#), ♭3rd (A), 5th (C#), ♭7th (E), 9th (G#)

F#/Gb9
Dominant 9th

A
A#/Bb
B
C
C#/Db
D
D#/Eb
E
F
F#/Gb
G
G#/Ab

Chord Spelling
1st (F#), 3rd (A#), 5th (C#), b7th (E), 9th (G#)

213

F#/G♭maj11
Major 11th

Chord Spelling
1st (F#), 3rd (A#), 5th (C#), 7th (E#), 9th (G#), 11th (B)

F#/G♭maj13
Major 13th

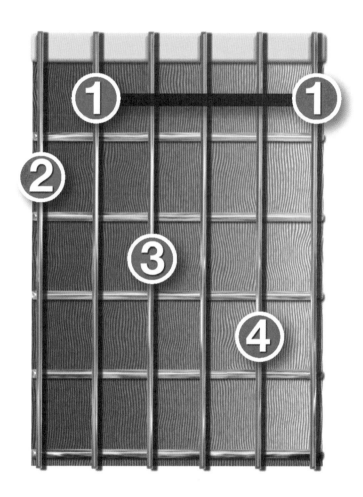

A
A#/B♭
B
C
C#/D♭
D
D#/E♭
E
F
F#/G♭
G
G#/A♭

Chord Spelling
1st (F#), 3rd (A#), 5th (C#), 7th (E#), 9th (G#), 11th (B), 13th (D#)

G
Major

Chord Spelling
1st (G), 3rd (B), 5th (D)

A

A#/B♭

B

C

C#/D♭

D

D#/E♭

E

F

F#/G♭

G

G#/A♭

Gm
Minor

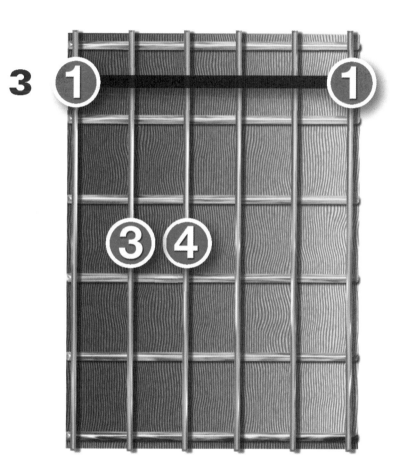

3

Chord Spelling
1st (G), ♭3rd (B♭), 5th (D)

A

A#/B♭

B

C

D#/E♭

D

E♭/D#

E

F

F#/G♭

G

G#/A♭

G+

Augmented Triad

Chord Spelling
1st (G), 3rd (B), ♯5th (D♯)

A

A♯/B♭

B

C

C♯/D♭

D

D♯/E♭

E

F

F♯/G♭

G

G♯/A♭

FREE ACCESS on smartphones
including iPhone & Android

Using any QR code app
scan and **HEAR** the chord

218

G°
Diminished Triad

X   X

2

Chord Spelling

1st (G), ♭3rd (B♭), ♭5th (D♭)

A

A#/B♭

B

C

D#/E♭

D

E♭/D#

E

F

F#/G♭

G

G#/A♭

Gsus2
Suspended 2nd

Chord Spelling
1st (G), 2nd (A), 5th (D)

A
A#/Bb
B
C
C#/Db
D
D#/Eb
E
F
F#/Gb
G
G#/Ab

Gsus4
Suspended 4th

Chord Spelling
1st (G), 4th (C), 5th (D)

G5
5th (Power Chord)

X X X

3

Chord Spelling
1st (G), 5th (D)

A
A#/Bb
B
C
C#/Db
D
D#/Eb
E
F
F#/Gb
G
G#/Ab

G6
Major 6th

Chord Spelling
1st (G), 3rd (B), 5th (D), 6th (E)

A
A#/Bb
B
C
D#/Eb
D
Eb/D#
E
F
F#/Gb
G
G#/Ab

Gm6
Minor 6th

3

Chord Spelling
1st (G), ♭3rd (B♭), 5th (D), 6th (E)

G6sus4
6th Suspended 4th

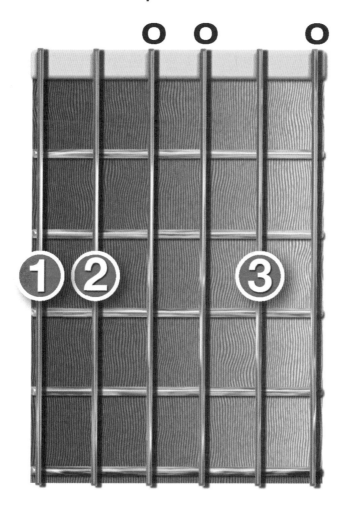

A

A#/Bb

B

C

D#/Eb

D

Eb/D#

E

F

F#/Gb

G

G#/Ab

Chord Spelling

1st (G), 4th (C), 5th (D), 6th (E)

Gmaj7
Major 7th

X   X

2

① ② ③ ④

Chord Spelling
1st (G), 3rd (B), 5th (D), 7th (F♯)

A
A♯/B♭
B
C
C♯/D♭
D
D♯/E♭
E
F
F♯/G♭
G
G♯/A♭

Gm7
Minor 7th

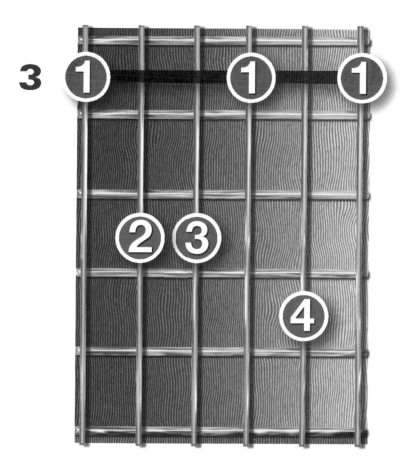

3

A
A#/B♭
B
C
D#/E♭
D
E♭/D#
E
F
F#/G♭
G
G#/A♭

Chord Spelling
1st (G), ♭3rd (B♭), 5th (D), ♭7th (F)

G7
Dominant 7th

Chord Spelling
1st (G), 3rd (B), 5th (D), ♭7th (F)

G°7
Diminished 7th

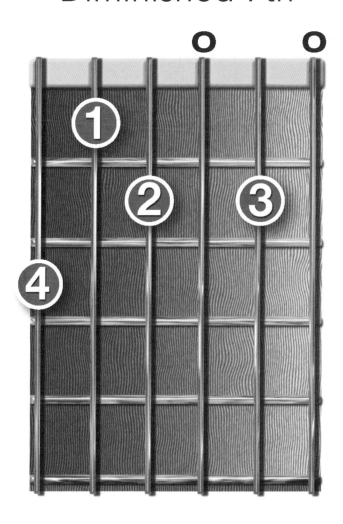

Chord Spelling
1st (G), ♭3rd (B♭), ♭5th (D♭), ♭♭7th (F♭)

G7sus4
Dominant 7th Suspended 4th

Chord Spelling
1st (G), 4th (C), 5th (D), ♭7th (F)

Gmaj9
Major 9th

X

Chord Spelling

1st (G), 3rd (B), 5th (D), 7th (F♯), 9th (A)

A

A#/B♭

B

C

D#/E♭

D

E♭/D#

E

F

F#/G♭

G

G#/A♭

Gm9
Minor 9th

X X

① ② ③ ④

Chord Spelling
1st (G), ♭3rd (B♭), 5th (D), ♭7th (F), 9th (A)

G9
Dominant 9th

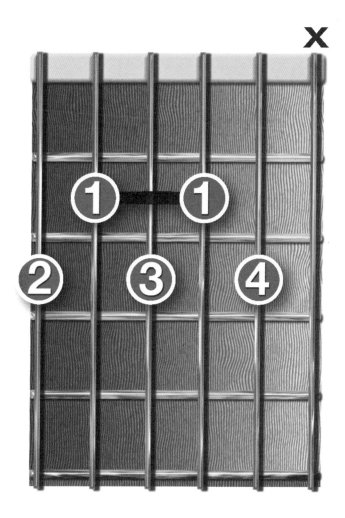

Chord Spelling
1st (G), 3rd (B), 5th (D), ♭7th (F), 9th (A)

FREE ACCESS on smartphones including iPhone & Android

Using any QR code app scan and **HEAR** the chord

233

A

A#/B♭

B

C

D#/E♭

D

E♭/D#

E

F

F#/G♭

G

G#/A♭

Gmaj11
Major 11th

Chord Spelling
1st (G), 3rd (B), 5th (D), 7th (F#), 9th (A), 11th (C)

234

Gmaj13
Major 13th

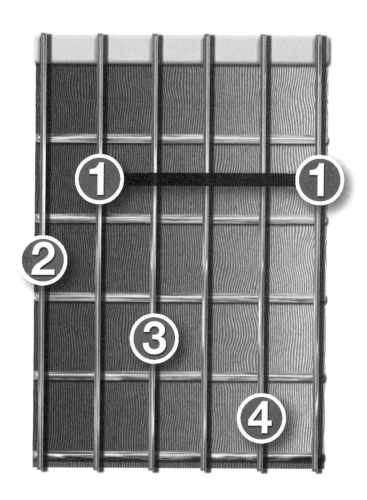

A

A#/Bb

B

C

D#/Eb

D

Eb/D#

E

F

F#/Gb

G

G#/Ab

Chord Spelling
1st (G), 3rd (B), 5th (D), 7th (F♯), 9th (A), 11th (C), 13th (E)

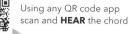

G♯/A♭
Major

Chord Spelling
1st (A♭), 3rd (C), 5th (E♭)

A

A♯/B♭

B

C

C♯/D♭

D

D♯/E♭

E

F

F♯/G♭

G

G♯/A♭

G♯/A♭m
Minor

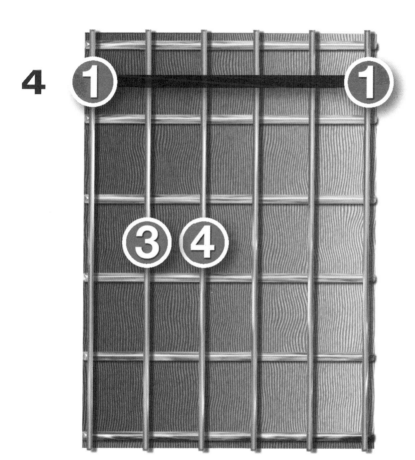

4

Chord Spelling
1st (A♭), ♭3rd (C♭), 5th (E♭)

A
A♯/B♭
B
C
C♯/D♭
D
D♯/E♭
E
F
F♯/G♭
G
G♯/A♭

G♯/A♭+
Augmented Triad

X X

① ② ③ ④

Chord Spelling
1st (A♭), 3rd (C), ♯5th (E)

A
A♯/B♭
B
C
C♯/D♭
D
D♯/E♭
E
F
F♯/G♭
G
G♯/A♭

G#/A♭°

Diminished Triad

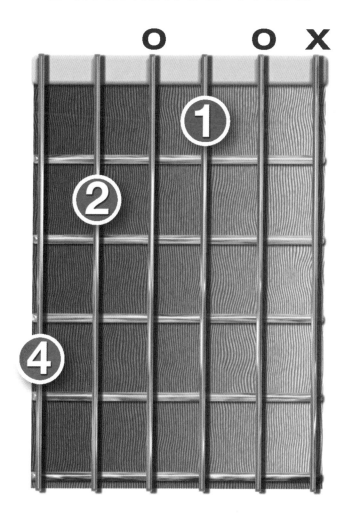

O   O   O   X

A

A#/B♭

B

C

C#/D♭

D

D#/E♭

E

F

F#/G♭

G

G#/A♭

Chord Spelling

1st (A♭), ♭3rd (C♭), ♭5th (E♭♭)

G#/A♭sus2
Suspended 2nd

Chord Spelling
1st (A♭), 2nd (B♭), 5th (E♭)

FREE ACCESS on smartphones
including iPhone & Android

Using any QR code app
scan and **HEAR** the chord

G#/A♭sus4
Suspended 4th

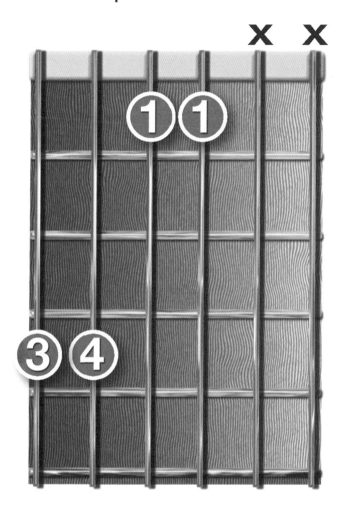

Chord Spelling
1st (A♭), 4th (D♭), 5th (E♭)

A
A#/B♭
B
C
C#/D♭
D
D#/E♭
E
F
F#/G♭
G
G#/A♭

G♯/A♭5

5th (Power Chord)

X X X

4 ① ③ ④

Chord Spelling
1st (A♭), 5th (E♭)

G#/A♭6
Major 6th

A

A#/B♭

B

C

C#/D♭

D

D#/E♭

E

F

F#/G♭

G

G#/A♭

Chord Spelling
1st (A♭), 3rd (C), 5th (E♭), 6th (F)

G#/A♭m6
Minor 6th

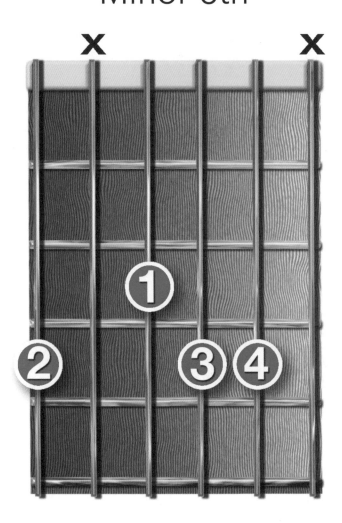

Chord Spelling
1st (A♭), ♭3rd (C♭), 5th (E♭), 6th (F)

FREE ACCESS on smartphones
including iPhone & Android

Using any QR code app
scan and **HEAR** the chord

A

A#/B♭

B

C

C#/D♭

D

D#/E♭

E

F

F#/G♭

G

G#/A♭

G♯/A♭6sus4
6th Suspended 4th

Chord Spelling

1st (A♭), 4th (D♭), 5th (E♭), 6th (F)

A
A♯/B♭
B
C
C♯/D♭
D
D♯/E♭
E
F
F♯/G♭
G
G♯/A♭

G#/A♭maj7
Major 7th

Chord Spelling
1st (A♭), 3rd (C), 5th (E♭), 7th (G)

A
A#/B♭
B
C
C#/D♭
D
D#/E♭
E
F
F#/G♭
G
G#/A♭

G♯/A♭m7
Minor 7th

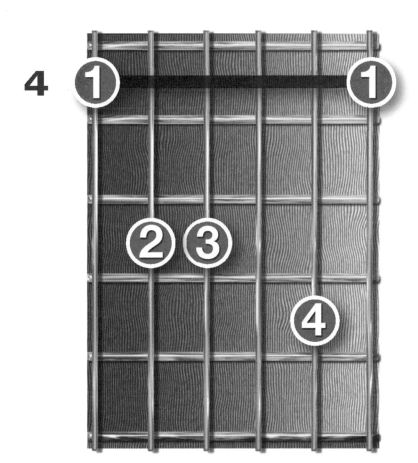

4

A
A♯/B♭
B
C
C♯/D♭
D
D♯/E♭
E
F
F♯/G♭
G
G♯/A♭

Chord Spelling
1st (A♭), ♭3rd (C♭), 5th (E♭), ♭7th (G♭)

FREE ACCESS on smartphones
including iPhone & Android

Using any QR code app
scan and **HEAR** the chord

G#/Ab7
Dominant 7th

Chord Spelling
1st (Ab), 3rd (C), 5th (Eb), b7th (Gb)

G#/A♭°7
Diminished 7th

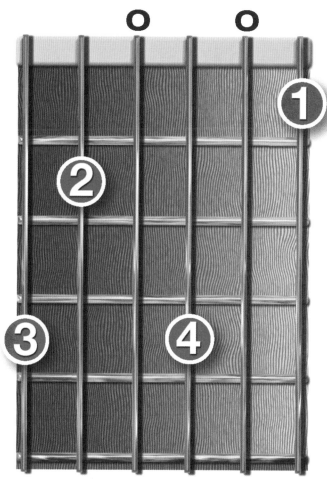

Chord Spelling
1st (A♭), ♭3rd (C♭), ♭5th (E♭♭), ♭♭7th (G♭♭)

A

A#/B♭

B

C

C#/D♭

D

D#/E♭

E

F

F#/G♭

G

G#/A♭

G♯/A♭7sus4
Dominant 7th Suspended 4th

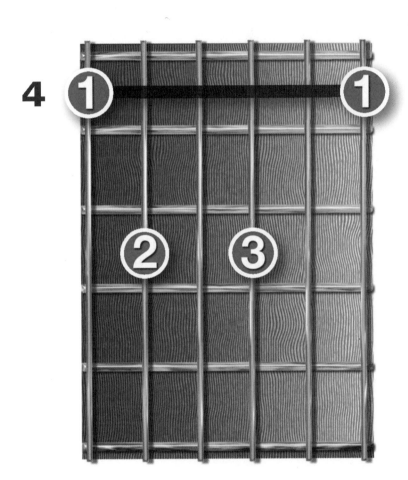

A
A♯/B♭
B
C
C♯/D♭
D
D♯/E♭
E
F
F♯/G♭
G
G♯/A♭

4

Chord Spelling
1st (A♭), 4th (D♭), 5th (E♭), ♭7th (G♭)

G♯/A♭maj9
Major 9th

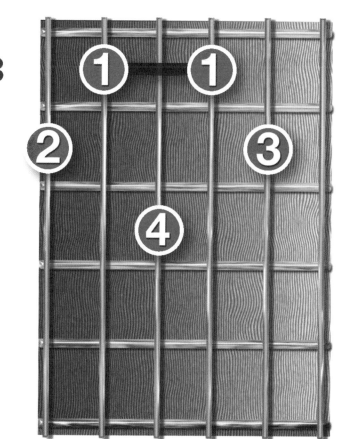

3

X

Chord Spelling
1st (A♭), 3rd (C), 5th (E♭), 7th (G), 9th (B♭)

A

A♯/B♭

B

C

C♯/D♭

D

D♯/E♭

E

F

F♯/G♭

G

G♯/A♭

G#/A♭m9
Minor 9th

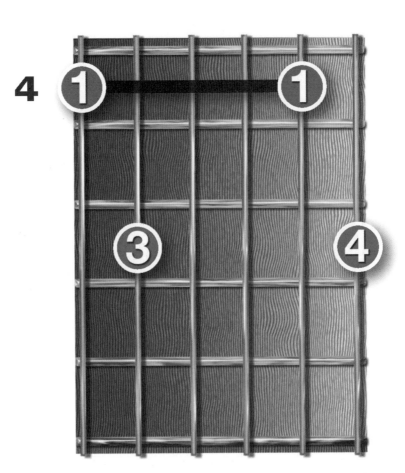

A
A#/B♭
B
C
C#/D♭
D
D#/E♭
E
F
F#/G♭
G
G#/A♭

4

Chord Spelling
1st (A♭), ♭3rd (C♭), 5th (E♭), ♭7th (G♭), 9th (B♭)

G♯/A♭9

Dominant 9th

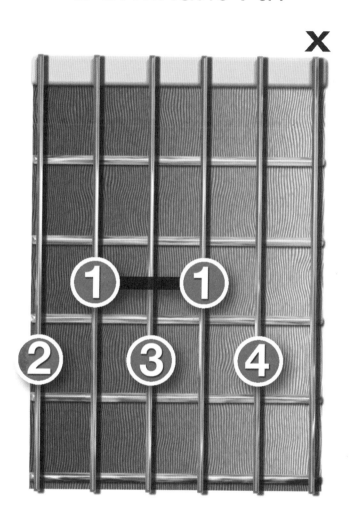

Chord Spelling

1st (A♭), 3rd (C), 5th (E♭), ♭7th (G♭), 9th (B♭)

G#/A♭maj11
Major 11th

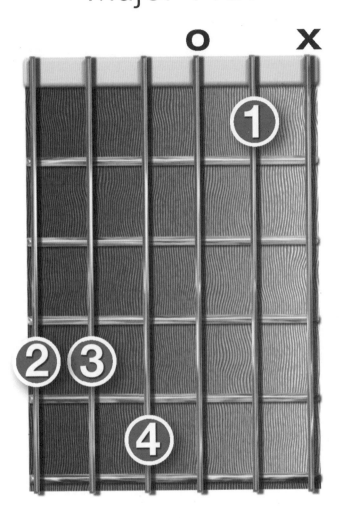

O   X

Chord Spelling

1st (A♭), 3rd (C), 5th (E♭), 7th (G), 9th (B♭), 11th (D♭)

Sidebar notes:
A
A#/B♭
B
C
C#/D♭
D
D#/E♭
E
F
F#/G♭
G
G#/A♭

G#/Abmaj13
Major 13th

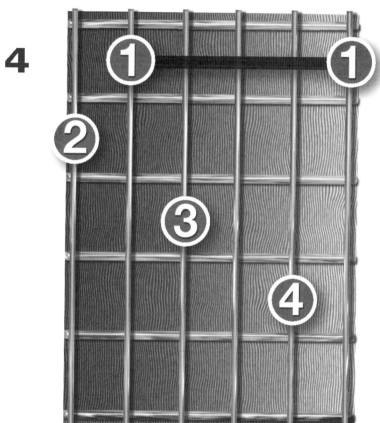

4

A
A#/Bb
B
C
C#/Db
D
D#/Eb
E
F
F#/Gb
G
G#/Ab

Chord Spelling
1st (Ab), 3rd (C), 5th (Bb), 7th (G), 9th (Bb), 11th (Db), 13th (F)

GUITAR CHORDS MADE EASY

A new title in our best-selling series, designed for players of all abilities and ages. Created for musicians by musicians, these books offer a quick and practical resource for those playing on their own or with a band. They work equally well for the rock and indie musician as they do for the jazz, folk, country, blues or classical enthusiast.

The MUSIC MADE EASY series

See it and Hear it! Comprehensive sound links

Guitar Chords Made Easy, Piano and Keyboard Chords Made Easy, Scales and Modes Made Easy, Reading Music Made Easy, Learn to Play Piano Made Easy, Learn to Play Guitar Made Easy.

The SPIRAL, EASY-TO-USE series

Advanced Guitar Chords; Advanced Piano Chords; Guitar Chords; Piano & Keyboard Chords; Chords for Kids; Play Flamenco; How to Play Guitar; How to Play Bass Guitar; How to Play Classic Riffs; Songwriter's Rhyming Dictionary; How to Become a Star; How to Read Music; How to Write Great Songs; How to Play Rhythm, Riffs & Lead Rock; How to Play Hard, Metal & Nu Rock; How to Make Music on the Web; My First Recorder Music; Piano Sheet Music; Brass & Wind Sheet Music; Scales & Modes; Beginners' Guide to Reading Music.

For further information on these titles please visit our trading website:
www.flametreepublishing.com

www.flametreemusic.com

Practical information on chords, scales, riffs, rhymes and instruments through a growing combination of traditional print books and ebooks. Features over **1800 chords**, with **sound files** for notes and strummed chords.